PIANO • VOCAL • GUITAR

W9-BDG-502

THE PRINCESS DIARIES·2
ROYAL ENGAGEMENT

ISBN 0-634-08959-5

SEVEN PEAKS MUSIC

DISTRIBUTED BY

HAL•LEONARD®
CORPORATION

7777 W. BLUEMOUND RD. P.O. BOX 13819 MILWAUKEE, WI 53213

Visit Hal Leonard Online at
www.halleonard.com

BREAKAWAY

Words and Music by BRIDGET BENENATE,
AVRIL LAVIGNE and MATTHEW GERRARD

I DECIDE

Words and Music by
DIANE WARREN

Don't think _ that you _ can tell _ me what _ to think. _
- er gon - na hold _ me down. _

I'm the one _ who knows _ what's good _ for me. _
Could - n't do _ it then, _ can't do _ it now. _

THIS IS MY TIME

Words and Music by MATTHEW GERRARD,
ROBBIE NEVIL and RAVEN SYMONE

Moderately fast

* *Recorded a half step lower.*

I ALWAYS GET WHAT I WANT

Words and Music by AVRIL LAVIGNE
and CLIF MAGNESS

Recorded a half step lower.

TROUBLE

Words and Music by ALECIA B. MOORE
and TIM ARMSTRONG

Driving Rock

No at-tor-neys_ to plead my

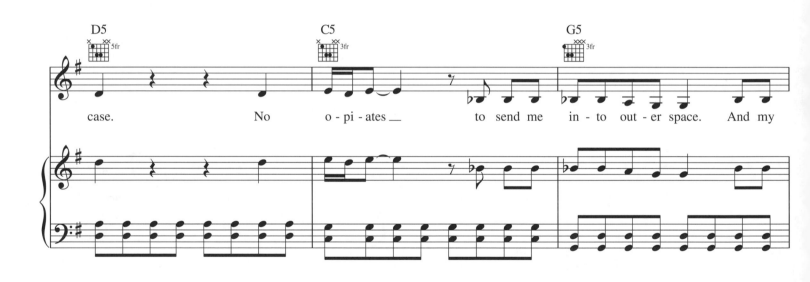

case. No o-pi-ates_ to send me in-to out-er space. And my

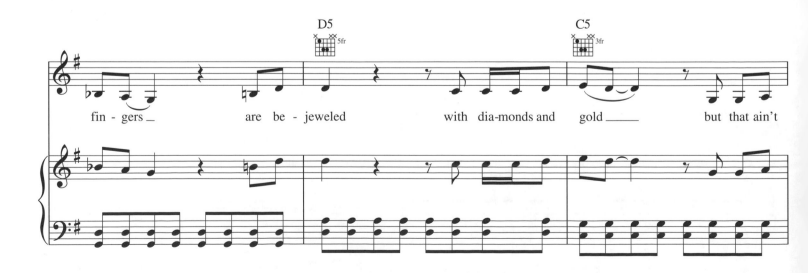

fin-gers_ are be-jeweled with dia-monds and gold _____ but that ain't

BECAUSE YOU LIVE

Words and Music by DESMOND CHILD,
ANDREAS CARLSSON and CHRIS BRAIDE

LOVE ME TENDER

Words and Music by ELVIS PRESLEY
and VERA MATSON

FUN IN THE SUN

Words and Music by MATTHEW GERRARD,
ROBBIE NEVIL and STEVEN HARWELL

LET'S BOUNCE

Words and Music by MATTHEW GERRARD
and ROBBIE NEVIL

DANCE, DANCE, DANCE

Words and Music by BRIAN WILSON,
CARL WILSON and MIKE LOVE

FOOLS

Words and Music by KAREN ANN POOLE,
ARNTHOR BIRGISSON, HENRIK JANSON and ANDERS BAGGE

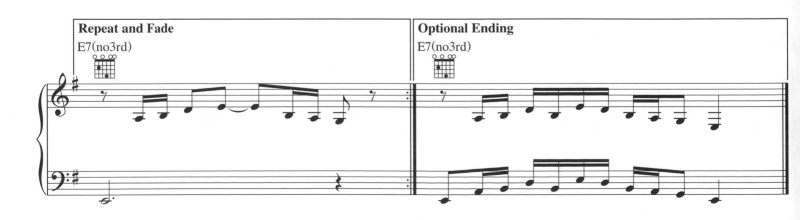

A LOVE THAT WILL LAST

Words and Music by DAVID FOSTER
and LINDA THOMPSON

YOUR CROWNING GLORY

Words and Music by LORRAINE FEATHER
and LARRY GROSSMAN

MIRACLES HAPPEN

Words and Music by ELIOT KENNEDY
and PAM SHEYNE

(Foreign lyrics)

(Foreign lyrics continue)

(Foreign lyrics continue)

(Foreign lyrics continue)

You showed me faith ____ is ____ not blind. __

__ I don't need wings ____ to help __ me fly. ____ Mir - a - cles hap-